*To Val & Kyle
much Love
— Joe*

poems
by
joe

Joseph L. Booze

joe booze

authorHOUSE

AuthorHouse™
1663 Liberty Drive, Suite 200
Bloomington, IN 47403
www.authorhouse.com
Phone: 1-800-839-8640

© 2008 Joe Booze. All rights reserved.

No part of this book may be reproduced, stored in a retrieval system, or transmitted by any means without the written permission of the author.

First published by AuthorHouse 10/15/2008

ISBN: 978-1-4389-1753-5 (sc)

Printed in the United States of America
Bloomington, Indiana

This book is printed on acid-free paper.

This book of poems is dedicated to my best friend and wife of forty-seven years and counting, Veronica P. Booze (Ronnie).

Contents

Poems By Joe ~ iii
Prologue ~ viii
Buzz the Bee ~ 1
Growing Near ~ 2
Their God ~ 3
Birdseed ~ 4
Christine and Lilly ~ 5
My Poems ~ 6
Meet the Press ~ 7
The Light of Day ~ 8
Excitement ~ 9
The Water Hole ~ 10
Spoken Words ~ 11
Friendship ~ 12
The N Word ~ 13
Home ~ 14
The Traveler ~ 15
"Morning Cup" ~ 16
"Those among Us" ~ 17
Heaven Sent ~ 18
The Player ~ 19
The Baby ~ 20
My New Bag ~ 21
Shanghai Volunteers ~ 22
The Nightly Hunt ~ 23
A Journey East ~ 24
Darkness ~ 25
Jena 6 (Louisiana) ~ 26
Shanghai ~ 27
A Dog's Tail ~ 28
Let's Play ~ 29
Places to Go ~ 30
My Sister Dorothy ~ 31
The Appointment ~ 32
When the Time Comes ~ 33
Madness ~ 34

All Grown up ~ 35
The Neighborhood ~ 36
Moving Forward ~ 37
The Cell Phone ~ 38
The Golfer ~ 39
The Fly ~ 40
Fat Cat ~ 41
Time Flies ~ 42
Military Daughter's Prayer ~ 43
Some People ~ 44
Who is an American ~ 45
Signs of the Times ~ 46

Prologue

It all started when this bee would not leave me alone while I was playing a round of golf. After returning home, I told Ronnie (my wife) what had happened, and she was very amused at what had happened and suggested that I should write a poem or short story about the bee. Story writing seems like a lot of work, so I decided to go the poem route.

Buzz the Bee

Old Buzz left the beehive to be on his own,
but for the life of him, he couldn't
leave people alone.

He loved to buzz around your head,
buzzing some crazy song, and got the nerve
to expect you to sing along.

It's no use telling Buzz you are not a singer,
because with a smile he'll point to his stinger.

Now if you ever were stung by a bee,
you know it hurts really bad, so it wouldn't
be smart to make old Buzz mad.

Buzz isn't a bad bee, as bees go,
but he's a little pushy and needs to take it slow.

There are a lot of birds out here
that wouldn't put up with Buzz's mess
and wouldn't think twice about taking him
to their nest.

Buzz needs help; this we all know,
but who's going to tell him so?

Maybe someone can go to the beehive
and talk to the queen bee, to tell Old Buzz to let us be.

Now the Queen told us, and it ain't funny,
but Buzz has been high for some time on day-old honey.

Growing Near

She does not sound the same as before;
could this be a sign that angels
are calling for her at heaven's door?

At times like this, I never know the right
things to say, but being a friend of the angels,
maybe they will grant me a wish and keep
her due date a bit at bay.

There is no need to tell them about her undying love
and what she means to us all, because if their records
did not reflect such, they wouldn't be the ones
making the call.

Their God

Isn't it amazing that when the inevitable happens
on this earth and damage is done, some say
that it is due to man's sin; that it is something God has done.

I would like to meet their God, to see what
turns him on and gives him joy to bring
about such hurt during earthquakes, great fires,
and cyclones.

I always thought of these things as a normal
fact of life, occurring somewhere
on this earth on any given day, not someone's
God at work, making man pay.

When I see people suffering and dying
or children burned, no way are they going to
convince me that some God has done this
just to make man learn.

As a child I was told of a God that is loving
and caring and has my best interest at heart.
I think I'll stay with this one and keep the
other God apart.

Birdseed

They toss their words about like
seeds for hungry birds, to feed
those that are empty and craving
the word.

They speak with such authority,
using powerful, motivating words,
with the help of microphones;
and picture screens to ensure
they are seen and heard.

They used to talk about hell, faith,
and the heavenly gate, but now
their words are all about political
matters and those of race.

When did they stray away from
their calling, if they were ever called,
to speak about matters that they seem
to know nothing about at all?

The empty need to go elsewhere
to find the food they need; the only
thing they will get from these
speakers is more birdseed.

Christine and Lilly

My daughter and her dog are quite a pair;
who controls whom is still up in the air.
As I watch, the two of them go through
their playful routine; it's the funniest
sight I have ever seen.

Get the ball, Lilly; go, Lilly, go; what's
the problem? Why so slow? Watch me
fetch it; I'll show you what you are to do.
When I return, then it will be up to you.

As you can see, I didn't have to run very far,
nor very fast. Please pay attention when
I am talking to you, and stop digging in the grass.

Now that's really impolite, turning your head and
sticking your nose in the air as if you don't care.
If you think I am fetching the ball again, you have
another thought coming, and you can stop smacking
your lips; you ain't funny.

My Poems

My poems are like my family,
who are loving and caring, ready
to reach out, not afraid of sharing.

When I read my poems, I let the words
freely flow, allowing them to touch
a heart or two as they go.

I love to see the looks on faces,
especially when there's a smile;
I know then that the words have
awakened a good feeling deep inside.

Sometimes the smiles may be joined
by tears, but that's okay, because when
you allow words to enter your heart, it
heeds all the words that have been said.

While reading and seeing the smiles and
tears upon your face, I know that I
must hurry to write again to take others to
this joyous place.

Meet the Press

I sent my poems off with so much pride,

but after hearing what was to become

of them, I was horrified. A bit sad because

they were sent with such high hopes,

but the way they were to be displayed

struck me as a joke. I asked they be returned;

not to sit and moan; many have said

they are good poems and want to take

them home. It was their first trip

to a publisher, and I was not

impressed with the people they met.

They seem to have had no interest in the words,

only the money, and a rush to their press.

The Light of Day

Without the light of day, you may not see the flowers
and all the beautiful colors they display.

Without the light of day, you may hear the birds
but not see them as they gracefully fly away.

Without the light of day, you may not see a friend
smile while the two of you are at play.

Without the light of day, you may feel the snow
upon your face but not see all its wonder before
it melts away.

But one thing you will always see, even without
the light of day, is a clear path to heaven when Jesus
washes your sins away.

Excitement

What can it be; signs everywhere with the names
of McCain, Obama, and Hillary.
What a scene; laughing and joking while waiting
for their turns at the voting machine.

But something seemed to happen to them after they cast
their vote. They all reappeared as if someone had played
a very bad joke. We may never know what changed
their moods, but there alone; maybe they realized
that this isn't a laughing matter, that things must improve.

The Water Hole

While walking in the desert with Grace and Bryce
today, Grace was doing just fine and was happily at play.
But when we came to this water hole and Grace was told
not to walk therein; that's when all the screaming
began.

She screamed so loudly for all to hear; even the birds
from miles around flew away in fear. She screamed
for her mom because Papa Joe said no, and said she'd
had enough of the desert and wanted to go.

When she returned home still screaming at the top of her
lungs, she then told her mom what Papa Joe had done.
But when her mom asked her why her shoes were all wet,
She screamed even more and said, "That's what started
all this mess."

Spoken Words

When the words of love were spoken,
you were there, then, promising
each other never to forget as they were
softly spoken again and again.

The power of those words has brought
you to this point, even replacing some
things from the past you no longer
need or want.

You've allowed these precious love words
to go deep within, sheltering them like
precious gold, making a solemn promise
to increase their value as the two of you
grow old.

Always think back to the beginning,
remembering those words—*when*
and *where*—never forgetting the
uncontrollable joy and warm love
you both felt while there.

Friendship

Love and prayers are needed without delay
the Spirit of Darkness has attacked this dear friend,
and it must be driven away.

The fight may be long and hard, but don't despair;
the Spirit of Darkness will weaken more the more you care.
Bring strong love, because this spirit does not fight
fair; it will test more than once the love you share.

You must be willing to stay in the battle as long
at it may take; this dear friend we fight for has
a lot at stake. His family is waiting one by one
for his joyful return; therefore, you must not falter
until victory is won.

The Spirit of Darkness will not leave on its own accord,
so fight hard for this dear friend with all the strength
and love you can afford.

The N Word

The N word is still used by some
allowing it to slip easily from their
tongue; sadly they are unaware, or don't care,
that this word was sung before many
were hung.

When the N word is used, it's honoring
its creators, who couldn't be contained
as they danced and cheered while
causing so much hurt and pain.

Years have passed, and many of these
wicked men and women have long
gone to their graves to stand before
the maker, but I doubt if any will
be saved.

This one word has so many meanings,
all of which are very demeaning,
and it doesn't matter how or in what
form the N word is used. You bring
disrespect to those who were and are abused.

Home

While taking a rest on the trail alone, for no apparent
reason I turned over this stone. To my surprise this
bug screamed out, *"What f I turned over your home?"*
Before I could say I didn't mean any harm,
he was already walking up my arm.

I tried to keep him in view, because this was something
I had never seen. He was wearing these big, fuzzy, red
slippers and carrying this rolled-up magazine.

He didn't say a word, just whacked me across the nose.
and motioned with his magazine that I should find
another place to enjoy the forest scene. Wide eyed
and shocked, giving him no lip, I replaced the stone
that was his home very carefully with a gentle flip.

The Traveler

The roads you travel will have many turns,
but no matter which one you take, there's
a lesson to be learned. Start your journey
wisely, because all roads are not clear;
watch for danger signs, because they will appear.

Be aware of those roads that are marked
"One Way"; you may not be able to turn
in time before a toll must be paid. Use the light
you carry wisely; don't allow it to fade; you must
be able to see the potholes and the steep
hills we all dread

Seek help from the Traveler; he will always
be near, because if your map was misprinted,
he will show you which roads are free and
those requiring a heavy fee. The roads of life
have many turns, but no matter which one you take,
there's a lesson to be learned.

"Morning Cup"

Why are they grinning and staring at me?
Can't they see I just want to read the
morning paper while sipping my coffee.

Even after turning a bit toward the door,
Is it my imagination? Their grinning
and staring seem to be worse than
before.

Who are these people; they are strangers
to me; why don't they stop all the grinning
and staring so I can drink my coffee?

Would you believe they are up and walking
my way. Not knowing them, what on earth
could they possibly have to say?

Well I'll be darned, they walked right by, to a
lady holding a baby humming a soft lullaby.
Now I'm grinning and staring as they did before.
Is it my imagination, or did that person over there
just turn his chair towards the door?

"Those among Us"

On any given day, just up the road
a way, you won't believe what you
will see. But I'm here to tell you,
it always surprises me.

I'm standing here looking at a sofa,
a stove, and a broken TV, plus old, dead
palm trees and piles of trash. I bet that
old car over there, when new, cost a lot of cash.

What sort of people would
do this to this land? Are they lacking
in pride, having no shame? I would love to
be near, should they be caught, as they
explained their twisted thoughts.

Week after week students from
Bailey Middle School gather here
with their large yellow plastic bags
to do their best to clean up this
senseless mess.

It's sad we have people living among
us that show such lack of taste and
dump trash all over this place. It
wouldn't be bad if they had no other
way, but who among us hasn't
heard of trash pickup day?

Note: This was written in honor of the students at Bailey Middle School that participated in their school cleanup project on East Lake Mead Boulevard, approximately one mile east of Hollywood Boulevard

Heaven Sent

It's falling from heaven so clear and warm,
a welcome sight during this gentle storm.

We have been without rain for such a long
time, so why would anyone complain
or whine?

Let's hope enough will keep falling to water all
the flowers and trees, plus much more to
fill other dry needs.

Look up to heaven, let it fall softly upon
your face, dance with joy as it dampens
this dry place.

While looking to heaven on this rare rainy
day, pray that it will keep falling and falling
on this blessed day.

The Player

He appeared at the clubhouse dressed like a pro,
with his glove sticking out his rear pocket, all
set to go.

He paid his green fee and adjusted his hat
and walked out of the clubhouse and straight to
the starter's shack.

His clubs were waiting for him, neatly loaded
on his cart.
So he wasted no time telling everyone
he was ready to start.

He noticed he was one of four that he had
played with before, so with a smile he thought
he would turn in the lowest score.

After hitting his ball in the rough on number
one, he just blamed it on the sun. Two,
three, and four were about the same. The way
he was playing was an awful shame.

By the time he got to number eight, he was ready to
throw his clubs in the lake. It all happened so
quickly, from number one to eight, but with ten
holes to go, maybe it was not too late.

I was told that when he returned to the clubhouse
to post his score, he was very calm and left
with a bit of charm. He came like a pro and departed
like a pro.
But he left everyone wondering, *Where did his clubs go?*

The Baby

Nestled in my mother's arms, free from care,
protected from harm, listening to her heart—
Oh! What a beautiful song.

I am not opening my eyes to see who else is near.
Instead let me find another position, a foot there,
an arm here, maybe my head just a bit near.

I heard someone say my daddy is waiting for me
to open my eyes. I shouldn't keep him waiting, but
Mom just started another lullaby.

With the sound of her voice and the rhythm of her
heart, it's so hard for me to open my eyes so dad
can play his part. But when I'm in his arms and listening
to his heart, I hear him sing sometimes;
let's hope he doesn't start.

My New Bag

When the cell phone rang
I gave it no thought; I reached
into the pocketbook I'd just bought.

Still driving with one hand one the wheel
and the other in the pocketbook
this officer pulled me over
like I was a bigtime crook.

Now what did I do that was all that bad,
except trying to locate my cell phone in my
newly bought bag.

With the window down, and sitting erect,
I braced myself for the full effect.

He approached my car with book in hand
and had that same darn smile I saw
on Mickey's face at Disneyland.

Shanghai Volunteers

They were the sons and daughters
of Shanghai's best, who put true
love to the test.

Every morning, with smiles
on their faces, they returned
to their appointed places.

How can we forget what they
have done? Without them, the
games would not have been fun.

The Shanghai volunteers
gladly showed up every day
to get us to and from the games
without delay.

Coaches, staff, and athletes from
all over the world will remember these
volunteers as if they were precious
Chinese pearls.

Note: Written in honor of the volunteers in Shanghai, China that assisted at the 2007 World Games held for athletes with intellectual disabilities.

The Nightly Hunt

Like a hungry cat after prey, she must
stay in the hunt, not allowing any to get away.

The streets are so dark, but the corners are bright,
so to catch her prey, she must remain there
in the light.

Soon the prey will appear out of the dark, driving
really slow; she must move quickly; it must not
be allowed to go.

When she stepped into his world and was told
what he wants, she become the prey, no longer
in charge of the hunt.

Night after night, the prey and the hunter
play this dangerous game, keeping alive the oldest
hunt that always ends in pain.

A Journey East

They flew to the Far East on a journey in time
to join other athletes to become one in body
and mind.

The goals they seek may not bring victory, but
none will come and go without making history.

When they assemble in Shanghai Stadium to
take their places, angels in heaven will make
a golden notation.

Before returning home, whence they came,
they should have met numerous
friends and obtained great fame.

What other group do you know of that can leave
and return as champions, other than
our wonderful Olympians.

Note: Written in honor of all the athletes from the United States
that participated in the 2007 World Games held in Shanghai, China
for athletes with intellectual disabilities.

Darkness

The darkness will soon be coming,
blocking those things that were
once clear and sunny.
There will be a chill in the air,
spreading all about, making the darkness
feel fearful and full of fright.
You won't see it coming because its way
is never clear; you must be on guard as it
approaches near.
Some will have enough light to see the way
clear, but many others will stumble and fall
in fear.
What are you doing to brighten your way
when the cloud of darkness comes on that
unclear day?
Will your light be bright enough
for you to see clear, showing there's
nothing in the darkness for you to fear?

Jena 6 (Louisiana)

It's hard to believe in this day and age
that racial hatred still has the nerve
to raise its ugly head.

Blacks and whites are beaten, and their
towns are torn apart; how on earth was
this allowed to start?

Although sadly it happened in the South,
is this sickness all about?

Imagine returning home after fighting
for the Land Of the Free and being told
you are not welcome to sit under this darn tree.

We are spending millions attempting
to communicate with outer space;
will they be warned of this racial hate?

Blacks and whites alike have marched and died
to rid us of this shame, but now in this day and age
we must sadly reflect on these words and
whence they came: "Free at last, free at last,
thank God almighty, we are free at last."
Now the question remains, with a great deal of pain.
Are we?

Shanghai

Shanghai, Shanghai with your buildings so tall,
let the sun come through; daylight calls.

Your children will soon be awake and will want to
play to get ready for World Games day.

All Shanghai will want to know how they will do
in swimming; running, or golf, just to name a few.

Many will be there from all over this great land
to cheer when they take the victory stand.

Shanghai, Shanghai, quickly push away the clouds;
let the sun come through. We want your children
to be the best at what they are about to do.

Note: Written in honor of all the Chinese athletes that participated in the 2007 World Games held for athletes with intellectual disabilities.

A Dog's Tail

There was a dog who thought he lost his tail.

He asked the duck, but got just a quack;
he then asked a beaver, who said, "I'm busy,
but I'll be right back."

Without an answer from his friends,
he felt this must be the end. Depressed
and saddened by the thought of losing his tail,
he jumped the fence and ran up the trail.

He met a man selling tails,
but with no money, there wasn't a sale.

He ran to the river to end it all,
but the reflection from the water
showed he hadn't lost his tail at all.

Let's Play

Look at all these things: climbing bars,
a merry-go-round, and swings.
Don't just stand there; let's go play.
You think we have all day?

But before we play, let me tell you
a few things. The swings are okay,
but the sliding board gets so hot
you can fry fish right there, on the spot.

Be careful when you roll and play in the grass.
grownups come here at night and make
noise and break glass. Also, don't play in the sand.
The stuff the dogs leave, you don't want to touch
with your hands.

You see all that stuff written all about?
Don't try to read it; it's something called graffiti.
I don't know what it's supposed to say;
it keeps getting painted over, but it's right back
the next day.

Well, let's go play and try to have fun and not think
of all the bad stuff someone's done.
We'd better hurry; the baby is awake and mom's off the
cell phone, and soon she'll be calling for us to go home.

Places to Go

You ever wonder where your dog goes when
he's asleep?

You think he goes to China to climb
the Great Wall or hops a train to New York
to leap over Niagara Falls?

Maybe he doesn't go anywhere but stays
right there at home to keep an eye on his
favorite bone.

He will never tell where he's been, but you know
he had fun; just look at that grin.

Tonight when I go to sleep, I'm going to have fun too.
I'm going to Disneyland and the San Diego
Zoo.

When I wake in the morning and he sees the grin on my face,
He will wonder too, *Where has she been,*
for goodness' sake?

My Sister Dorothy

I have a sister that I want you all to know
because she's such a sweet person
and you can't help but love her so.

I believe that when God made her, he may
have broken the mold, because you will
be hard pressed to find another
with such a heart of gold

Although she's been ill for such a long
time, you would never know it, because
she never complains or whines.

What a wonderful sister she's always
been; the old stork would be hard pressed
to bring a mom and dad such a sweet child again.

I'm deeply sorry I can't visit her
but once a year, but by sending
cards and letters and calling her by
phone, I try to keep her near.

For those of you who haven't met her,
do so before it's too late, because when God
calls her home, she's going though the
Precious Children's Gate.

The Appointment

When we walked into the office, there was a chill in the air,
and there sat the dentist's chair.

When she went with the dentist to take her seat,
I was sure happy they were not my teeth.

Soon the sound of the drill had me on the edge of my seat,
and from where I sat, I could see her feet.

She wore open-toe shoes that day,
and I could see her toes slowly curling up a ways.

With the sound of the drill and the hissing of air,
I then saw her feet slowly rising in the air.

Soon I could hear moans and screams,
and then I saw the wildest leg-kicking I had ever seen.

After what seemed like an hour, the drilling stopped,
And I saw her toes uncurl and her legs slowly drop.

After a moment's pause, she appeared at the door,
holding a new toothbrush in her hand,
and without a word or smile, we left the same way we came.

When the Time Comes

Many of us have lost close friends,
family members, mothers, and fathers.

Tomorrow was not promised,
and we should understand it so,
understanding that just like our loved ones,
tomorrow may be our time to go.

The loved ones we lost were not here
for us to own; they were all children
belonging to the Heavenly Farther,
and the Father decided to call them home.

Now, if you are a child of the Father,
you should understand what's been said and
never ever think of your loved ones as being dead.

They are alive in our hearts and minds
for us to always call near, and when the
Heavenly Father calls us home, we will
again see them clear.

Dwelling daily on self pity, sadness, and sorrow
will not solve a thing. Be of great joy, and thankful
that you are also a child of the King.

Madness

Why do they spray all over the place?
It's so ugly and shows lack of taste.

With paint red, purple, black, or green,
are they that desperate to be seen?

They must not be proud of what they display,
otherwise it would be done during the day.

Everywhere you look;
without respect for property, you, or me;
we are exposed to this ugly graffiti.

You think there is an illness that
blinds them from this shame,
preventing them from seeing
their real hurt and pain.

You can't help but see it on walls,
buildings, and trucks, and I'm sure
you will agree that this mess is a total disgust.

All Grown up

Now our daughter is off to collage to pursue her goal;
can anyone believe she's really this old?

I guess we all knew this moment in time
would appear;
God knows we will miss our little dear.

It's no more "Clean your room, stop the noise,"
or "Put away your toys now"; it's now,
"Watch out for those college boys."

Her little brother can use the computer
all he please,
but sadly, she won't be here for him to tease.

We are all so glad; we loved her so much each day,
and we pray this love will strengthen her
while she's away.

Now it's down to business; worldly things must wait.
All that matters now is her graduation date.

The Neighborhood

It so sad when a neighborhood dies.
At one time mothers joyfully cooked,
children played, and babies cried.

The empty houses are so still and cold.
I wonder what happened to all those goals.

I wonder who were the first to go
and those that left just to follow the flow.

It's so sad when a neighborhood dies;
the abandoned buildings seem to cry out in pain,
with their shutters closed as if to hide the shame.

I was away when my neighborhood died.
Wasn't there to see the first to go
and those that followed the flow.

I remember the happy times way back then,
but sadly this neighborhood, too,
will never rise again.

Moving Forward

Running; running from pain and despair,
but not just anywhere. The night is so dark,
but I can still see the star that's leading me afar.

I must keep moving; I can hear the sounds of
the hounds as my thoughts guide me,
northbound.

I'll need help along the way; I must remember
those safe places where I was told to stay.

If I'm caught and returned whence I came,
I'll be stripped, beaten, and driven to pain.

I must not look back; there is nothing there
for me to see; I must keep looking
forward, forward; dear God, I must be free.

The Cell Phone

Fumbling for the cell phone is driving me insane.
I'd better get over in the right-hand lane.

Looking straight ahead, not wanting to be unsafe;
Where is that cell phone, for goodness' sake?

At last I found it between the seats,
but by then there was no Beethoven; not so much as a beep.

I quickly looked to see who had called,
but I didn't recognize the number at all.

Red lights flashing from the rear
and those hand gestures from passing motorists
Oh, dear.

I pulled to the curb and came to a stop,
and wouldn't you know it? It's the same smiling cop.

The Golfer

A three-hundred-yard drive was nothing for him;
even chipping to the greens was just a fine trim.

But when it came to putting, that was another story;
there was something mysterious between him and glory.

When he struck the ball to make the putt,
the dear ball again went amuck.

On bended knees with head bowed in pure sorrow,
he very quietly said,

    "Dear God, please be with me tomorrow."

The Fly

There was a fly in my soup,
trying to eat the beans;
such a sight I have never seen.

As he held on to the corn to stay afloat,
he opened his mouth and began to choke.

As I watched the poor fly gasping for air
my soup was getting cold, plus beans,
corn, and juice were being flung everywhere.

How he got there I can only guess,
but wherever he came from,
there will be one fly less.

Fat Cat

This cat was in the kitchen, looking with a stare
at a mouse with a sophisticated flair.

He circled the mouse to get a better look,
but the mouse slid away like a smoothly running brook.

The temper rose within the cat, but the mouse thought
he was safe, because this cat was way too fat.

The mouse started dancing to his hole, acting cool,
thinking, *No problem; this cat's a fool.*

I understand his thoughts that day, but it's a shame
he didn't see the broom coming from the other way.

Time Flies

If time flies, then tell me, please,
on what day does it leave?

I'm really happy where I stand,
but I heard there's free candy in Wonderland.

I hope the trip won't take too long;
it would be sad if it's all gone.

Packing a few things would be a breeze:
an apple, an orange, even some crackers
and cheese.
Do you think my mom would be very mad
if I look one of her good plastic bags?

Why, I could fill it to the top,
and we could eat candy till we popped.

Oh, please tell me on what day time flies;
if you don't, I'll surely cry.

I'm sure the trip isn't free,
but how much can the price
be for a little girl just three?

Military Daughter's Prayer

Dear Father up above, please return quickly;
we need your love.

Churches are on every corner, and missionaries
praise you in song, but it doesn't seem to
stop all the wrong.

Hunger and war abound everywhere, but
world leaders just don't seem to care.

I know you said "Free Will" and that it is up to
man, but please hurry as fast as you can.

I'm just a child, but help me understand
why so many are dying in far-off lands.

My mom is hugging my best friend's mother with
a letter in her hand, and if it's like the one mom got,
I fear she won't be seeing her dad again.

Some People

Some people will come with smiles
others will come with a bit of rain,
but the ones you should watch out
for, are those that come with pain.

They really don't care about you or
those before, there seem to be no
meaning to their life, nor joy.

It's no use trying to change their ways
it's best to let them pass, because if you
allow their pain to enter your heart
there it will last.

I bet you can think of one or two that
have tried to hurt you in some way;
if this is so, then you understand there's
nothing more to say.

Who is an American

Who is an American; it's hard to see,
so many are here today just for the liberty.
Unaware of the price that's been paid
by those that were free, and those who
were slaves.

I know it's more than just waving the flag
or making a lot of noise July the fourth;
so to answer who is an American I must
give it some thought.

An American to me can be of any breed,
but must have one thing in common
and that's to be free. Willing to pay the price
that must be paid, to keep America and its
people free, and not enslaved.

Respecting the land and all its wonder, willing
to fight if necessary come hell or thunder.
Showing an understanding to those who are new,
and have proven they also respect the red, white,
and blue.

Signs of the Times

People watching can be such fun as they hurry
to finish this or that before the day is done.
Ladies walking by in tight jeans, smiling as they
do so, aware they have been seen.

Young men passing by in baggy pants exposing
their underwear in total disgust, with heavy
chains around their necks, which would lay a
Pack Mule in the dust.

Little children smiling as if aware their parents will
do anything to avoid a fuss, as they lead the poor
souls into Toys "R" Us

Young girls walking by in flip flops looking twice
their age, with bodies developed far beyond their stage.
Exposing body parts that should be against the law; but
then again, it's nothing I haven't seen before.

All that I have seen today I could have taken in stride,
but when grandma strolled by wearing all those
tattoos; it was time to say goodbye.